THE

FLORAL WREATH

OF

AUTUMN FLOWERS.

BY MRS. SOUTHEY

Sixth Edition.

DETROIT:
KERR, DOUGHTY & LAPHAM.

CONTENTS.

AUTUMN FLOWERS.

AUTUMN FLOWERS.

THOSE few pale Autumn flowers,
How beautiful they are!
Than all that went before,
Than all the Summer store,
How lovelier far!

And why? They are the *last*—
The last!—the last!—the last!
O, by that little word
How many thoughts are stirred
That sister of the past!

Pale flowers! pale, perishing flowers!
Ye're types of precious things;
Types of those bitter moments
That flit, like life's enjoyments,
On rapid, rapid wings;—

Last hours with parting dear ones,
(That time the fastest spends,)
Last tears, in silence shed,
Last words, half-utteréd,
Last looks of dying friends

Who but would fain compress
A life into a day?
The last day spent with one
Who, ere the morrow's sun,
Must leave us, and for aye?

O, precious, precious moments!
Pale flowers! ye're types of those,—
The saddest, sweetest, dearest,—

Because, like those, the nearest
  Is an eternal close.

Pale flowers! pale, perishing flowers!
  I woo your gentle breath;
I leave the Summer rose,
For younger, blither brows:
  Tell me of change and death!

MY GARDEN.

I LOVE my garden — dearly love
    That little spot of ground;
There's not, methinks, (though I may err
In partial pride,) a pleasanter
    In all the country round.

The smooth, green turf winds gently there,
    With no ungraceful bend,

Round many a bed and many a border,
Where, gayly grouped in sweet disorder,
  Young Flora's darlings blend.

Spring, Summer, Autumn. Of all three,
  Whose reign is loveliest there?
O, is not she who paints the ground,
When its frost-fetters are unbound,
  The fairest of the fair?

I gaze upon her violet beds,
  Laburnums, golden-tressed,
Her flower-spiked almonds, breathe perfume
From lilach and seringa bloom,
  And cry, "I love Spring best!"

But Summer comes, with all her pomp
  Of fragrance, beauty, bliss,
And, from amidst her bowers of roses,
I sigh, as purple evening closes,
  "What season equals this?"

That pageant passeth by. Comes next
    Brown Autumn in her turn:
O, not unwelcome cometh she;
The parchéd earth luxuriously
    Drinks from her dewy urn.

And she hath flowers, and fragrance to ,
    Peculiarly her own;
Asters of every hue; perfume
Spiced rich with clematis and broom,
    And mignionette late blown.

Then if some lingering rose I spy
    Reclining languidly,
Or the bright laurel's glossy green,
Dear Autumn, my whole heart, I ween,
    Leaps up for love of thee

O yes! I love my garden well,
    And find employment there,—
Employment sweet for many an hour

AUTUMN FLOWERS.

.n tending every shrub and flower
    With still unwearied care.

I prop the weakly, prune the rude,
    Scatter the various seeds,
Clear out intruders, yet of *those*
Oft sparing what the florist knows
    To be but gaudy weeds.

But when my task — my pleasant task —
    Is ended for the day, —
Sprinkled o'er every sun-bowed flower
The artificial evening shower, —
    Then oftentimes I stray,

(Inherent is the love of change
    In human hearts,) far, far
Beyond the garden gate, — the bound
That clips my little Eden round,
    Chance for my leading star, —

Through hollow lanes or coppice paths,
By hill or hawthorn fence,
O'er thymy commons, clover fields,
Where every step I take reveals
Some charm of sight or sense

The winding path brings suddenly
A rustic bridge in sight;
Beneath it, gushing brightly out,
The rivulet, where speckled trout
Leap in the circling light.

Pale water-lilies float thereon,
The Naiads' loveliest wreath;
The adders' tongues dip down to drink
The flag peers high above the brink,
From her long, slender sheath.

There, on the greensward, an old oak
Stands singly; one, I trow,
Whose mighty shadow spread as wide

When they were in their prime who die
A hundred years ago.

A single ewe, with her twin lambs,
Stands the gray trunk beside;
Others lie clustering in the shade,
Or down the windings of the glade
Are scattered far and wide.

Two mossy thorns, o'er yonder stile,
A bowery archway rise;
O, what a flood of fragrance thence
Breathes out! Behind that hazel fence
A flowering bean-field lies.

The shadowy path winds gently on
That hazel fence beneath;
The wild-rose and the woodbine there
Shoot up, festooning high in air
Their oft-entangled wreath

The path winds on, on either side
    Walled in by hedges high;
Their boughs so thickly arching over,
That scarce one speck you can discover—
    One speck of the blue sky.

A lovely gloom! It pleaseth me
    And lonely Philomel.
Hark! the enchantress sings; that strain
Dies with a tremulous fall;—again—
    O, what a gushing swell!

Darker and darker still the road,
    Scarce lit by twilight glances;
Darker and darker still—but see!
Yonder, on that young aspen-tree,
    A darting sunbeam dances.

Another gems the bank below
    With emeralds; into one
They blend—unite—one emerald sea;

And last, in all his majesty,
    Breaks through the setting sun.

And I am breathless, motionless,
    Mute with delight and love;
My very being seems to blend
With all around me—to ascend
    To the great Source above.

I feel I am a spark struck out
    From an eternal flame;
A part of the stupendous whole;
His work who breathed a deathless soul
    Into this mortal frame.

And *they* shall perish—all these things;
    Darkness shall quench this ball;
Death-throes this solid earth shall rive;
Yet I—frail thing of dust!—survive
    The final wreck of all.

"Wake up, my glory! lute and harp!"
    Be vocal every chord!
Lo! all his works in concert sing,
"Praise, praise to the Eternal King,"
    The Universal Lord!

O powerless will! O languid voice.
    Weak words! imperfect lays!
Yet could his works alone inspire
The feelings that attune my lyre
    To these faint notes of praise.

Not to the charms of tasteful art
    That I am cold or dull;
I gaze on all the graceful scene,
The clustering flowers, the velvet green,
    And cry, "How beautiful!"

But when to Nature's book I turn,—
    The page *she* spreads abroad,—
Tears, only to mine eyes that steal,

Bear witness that I see and feel
The mighty hand of God.

TO LITTLE MARY

I'm bidden, little Mary,
To write verses unto thee,
I'd fain obey the bidding,
If it rested but with me,
But the mistresses I'm bound to,
(Nine ladies hard to please,)
Of all their stores poetic
So closely keep the keys,
Tis only now and then,
By good luck, as we may say,
A couplet or a rhyme or two
Falls fairly in my way.

Fruit forced is never half so sweet
As that comes quite in season;

But some folks must be satisfied
  With rhyme, in spite of reason,
So, muses, all befriend me, —
  Albeit of help so chary, —
To string the pearls of poesy
  For loveliest little Mary.

And yet, ye pagan damsels,
  Not over-fond am I
To invoke your haughty favors —
  Your fount of Castaly;
I've sipped a purer fountain;
  I've decked a holier shrine;
I own a mightier mistress;
  O Nature, thou art mine.

And only to that well-head,
  Sweet Mary, I'll resort,
For just an artless verse or two, —
  A simple strain, and short, —
Befitting well a pilgrim

Way-worn with care and strife,—
To offer thee, young traveller,
In the morning track of life.

There's many a one will tell thee
'Tis all with roses gay;
There's many a one will tell thee
'Tis thorny all the way.
Deceivers are they, every one,
Dear child, who thus pretend:
God's ways are not unequal;
Make him thy trusted Friend,
And many a path of pleasantness
He'll clear away for thee,
However dark and intricate
The labyrinth may be.

I need not wish thee beauty,
I need not wish thee grace;
Already both are budding
In that infant form and face

I *will not* wish thee grandeur,
  I *will not* wish thee wealth;
But only a contented heart,
  Peace, competence, and health;
Fond friends to love thee dearly,
  And honest friends to chide,
And faithful ones to cleave to thee,
  Whatever may betide.

And now, my little Mary,
  If better things remain
Unheeded in my blindness,
  Unnoticed in my strain,—
I'll sum them up succinctly
  In "English undefiled,"—
My mother-tongue's best benison,—
  God bless thee, precious child!

"SUFFICIENT UNTO THE DAY IS THE EVIL THEREOF."

O, by that gracious rule
  Were we but wise to steer
On the wide sea of thought,
What moments, trouble-fraught,
  Were spared us here!

But we, (perverse and blind,)
  As covetous of pain,
Not only seek for more
Yet hidden, but live o'er
  The past again.

This life is callèd brief;
  Man on the earth but crawls
His threescore years and ten,—
At best fourscore,—and then
  The ripe fruit falls.

Yet, betwixt birth and death,
  Were but the life of man
By his *thoughts* measured,
To what an age would spread
  That little span!

There are who're born and die,—
  Eat, sleep, walk, rest between,
Talk, *act* by clockwork too;
So pass, in order due,
  Over the scene;—

With whom the past is *past*,
  The future, *nothing yet;*
And so, from day to day,
They breathe, till called to pay
  The last great debt.

Their life, in truth, *is* brief;
  A speck—a point of time,
Whether in good old age

Ending their pilgrimage,
  Or in its prime

But other some there are,
  (I call them not more wise,)
In whom the restless mind
Still lingereth behind,
  Or forward flies.

With *these*, things pass away;
  But past things are not dead;
In the heart's treasury,
Deep-hidden, dead they lie,
  Unwitheréd.

And there the soul retires
  From the dull things that are,
To mingle, oft and long,
With the time-hallowed throng
  Of those that were.

Then into life start out
  The scenes long vanishéd;
Then we behold again
The forms that have long lain
  Among the dead.

We seek their grasp of love,
  We meet their beaming eye;
We speak — the vision's flown,
Dissolving with its own
  Intensity.

Years rapidly shift on,
  (Like clouds athwart the sky,)
And lo! sad watch we keep,
When in perturbéd sleep
  The sick doth lie.

We gaze on some pale face,
  Shown by the dim watch-light;
Shuddering, we gaze, and pray,

And weep, and wish away
  The long, long night.

And yet minutest things,
  That mark time's tedious tread,
Are on the feverish brain,
With self-protracting pain,
  Deep minuted;—

The drops with trembling hand
  (Love-steadiéd) poured out;
The draught replenishéd,
The label oft re-read
  With nervous doubt;—

The watch, that ticks so loud;
  The winding it for one
Whose hand lies powerless;
And then the fearful guess,
  "Ere *this* hath run"

The shutter, half unclosed
  As the night wears away,
Ere the last stars are set, —
Pale stars! that linger yet
  Till perfect day; —

The morn, so oft invoked,
  That bringeth no relief;
From which, with sickening sight,
We turn, as if its light
  But mocked our grief!

O, never, after dawn,
  For us the east shall streak,
But we shall see again,
With the same thoughts as then,
  That pale day-break! —

The desolate awakening,
  When first we feel alone; —
"Dread memories" are these;

Yet who for heartless ease
  Would exchange one?

These are the soul's hid wealth—
  Relics embalmed with tears.
Or, if her curious eye
Searches futurity,—
  The depth of years,—

There (from the deck of youth)
  Enchanted land she sees;
Blue skies and sun-bright bowers
Reflected, and tall towers,
  On glassy seas.

But heavy clouds collect
  Over that bright-blue sky,
And rough winds rend the trees,
And lash those glassy seas
  To billows high.

And then, the last thing seen
  By that dim light may be
(With helm and rudder lost)
A lone wreck, tempest-tost,
  On the dark sea.

Thus doth the soul extend
  Her brief existence *here*
Thus multiplieth she
(Yea, to infinity)
  The short career

Presumptuous and unwise.
  As if the present sum
Were little of life's woe!
Why seeketh she to know
  Ills yet to come?

Look up, look up, my soul,
  To loftier mysteries!
Trust in his word to thee

Who saith, " All tears shall be
  Wiped from all eyes."

And when thou turnest back,
  (O, what can chain thee *here*?)
Seek out the isles of light
On " memory's waste " yet bright;
  Or, if too near.

To desolate plains they lie,
  All dark with guilt and tears,
Still, still retrace the past,
Till thou alight, at last,
  On life's first years.

There not a passing cloud
  Obscures the sunny scene;
No blight on the young tree;
No thought of what *may be*,
  Or what *hath been*.

There all is hope — *not* hope,
  For all things are possessed;
No — bliss without alloy,
And innocence and joy,
  In the young breast;

And all-confiding love,
  And holy ignorance,
Thrice blessed veil! soon torn
From eyes foredoomed to mourn
  For man's offence.

O, thither, weary spirit,
  Flee from this world defiled.
How oft, heart-sick and sore,
I've wished I were once more
  A little child!

THE TREATY.

NEVER tell me of loving by measure and weight,
As one's merits may lack or abound;
As if love could be carried to market, like skate,
And cheapened for so much a pound.

If it can, — if yours can, — let them have it who care;
You and I, friend, shall never agree;
Pack, and to market; be off with your ware;
It's a great deal too common for me.

Do ye linger and laugh? I'm sincere, I declare,
But belike over-hasty in thought;
If it suits ye to close with my terms as they are,
Well and good — but I won't bate a jot.

You must love me — we'll note the chief articles now,
To preclude all mistakes in our pact.

And I'll pledge ye, unmasked and beforehand, my
vow,
To give double for all I exact.

You must love me not only through "evil report,"
When its falsehood you know or divine,
But when, upon earth, I can only resort
To your heart as a voucher for mine.

You must love me — not my faults, but, in spite of
them, me,
For the very caprices that vex ye;
Nay, the more, should ye chance, as it's likely, to see
'Tis my special delight to perplex ye.

You must love me, albeit all the world I offend
With my follies, my feelings, conceit,
While assured (if you are not, all treaty must end)
That I never can stoop to deceit; —

While assured, as we must be, (or there, too, we
must part,)

That, were all the world leagued against you,
To loosen one hair of your hold on my heart
Would be more than "life's labors" could do.

You must love me, howe'er I may take things amiss,
Whereof you in all conscience stand clear;
And although, when you'd fain make it up with a kiss,
Your reward be a box on the ear.

You must love me not only when smiling and gay,
Complying, sweet-tempered, and civil,
But when moping, and frowning, and froward, or — to say
The thing plain out — as cross as the devil.

You must love me in all moods, — in seriousness, in sport, —
Under all change of circumstance, too;
part, or together, in crowd, or — in short,
You must love me because I love you.

ABJURATION.

THERE was a time, — sweet time of youthful folly, —
Fantastic woes I courted, feigned distress,
Wooing the veilèd phantom Melancholy
With passion, born, like Love, "in idleness."

And, like a lover, — like a jealous lover, —
I hid mine idol with a miser's art, —
Lest vulgar eyes her sweetness should discover, —
Close in the inmost chambers of mine heart.

And then I sought her, — oft in secret sought her,
From merry mates withdrawn and mirthful play, —
To wear away, by some deep, stilly water,
In greenwood haunt, the livelong summer day;

Watching the flitting clouds, the fading flowers,
The flying rack athwart the waving grass,
And murmuring oft, "Alack, this life of ours!
Such are its joys! so swiftly doth it pass!"

And then mine idle tears (ah, silly maiden !)
Bedropt the liquid grass like summer rain,
And sighs, as from a bosom sorrow-laden,
Heaved the light heart that knew no real pain.

And then I loved to haunt lone burial-places,
To pace the churchyard earth with noiseless tread
To pore in new-made graves for ghastly traces —
Brown, crumbling bones — of the forgotten dead ;

To think of passing-bells, of death and dying ;
'Twere good, methought, in early youth to die ;
So loved ! lamented ! in such sweet sleep lying,
The white shroud all with flowers and rosemary

Stuck o'er by loving hands ! But then 'twould grieve me
Too sore, forsooth ! the scene my fancy drew ;
I could not bear the thought to die and leave ye ;
And I have lived, dear friends, to weep for you

And I have lived to prove what "fading flowers,"—
  And life's best joys, and all we love and prize,—
What chilling rains, succeed the summer showers!
  What bitter drops wrung slow from elder eyes!

And I have lived to look on "death and dying,"
  To count the sinking pulse, the shortening breath,
To watch the last faint life-streak flying—flying—
  To stoop, to start, to be alone with death.

And I have lived to feign the smile of gladness,
  When all within was cheerless, dark, and cold;
When all earth's joy seemed mockery and madness
  And life more tedious than "a tale twice told."

And now,—and now,—pale, pining Melancholy!
  No longer veiled for me your haggard brow
In pensive sweetness, such as youthful folly
  Fondly conceited; I abjure ye now!

Away! avaunt! No longer now I call ye
  "Divinest Melancholy! mild, meek maid!"

No longer may your siren spells inthrall me,
  A willing captive in your baleful shade.

"Give me the voice of mirth, the sound of laughte
  The sparkling glance of Pleasure's roving eye;
The past is past; avaunt, thou dark hereafter!
  Come, eat and drink; to-morrow we must die."

So, in his desperate mood, the fool hath spoken,—
  The fool, whose heart hath said "there is no God;
But for the stricken soul—the spirit broken—
  There's balm in Gilead still. The very rod,

If we but kiss it as the stroke descendeth,
  Distilleth oil to allay the inflicted smart;
And "peace that passeth understanding" blendet
  With the deep sighing of the contrite heart.

Mine be that holy, humble tribulation,
  No longer "feigned distress, fantastic woe;"
I know my griefs; but then my consolation,
  My trust, and my immortal hopes, I know

TO A DYING INFANT.

Sleep, little baby, sleep;
Not in thy cradle bed,
Not on thy mother's breast,
Henceforth shall be thy rest,
But with the quiet dead.

Yes, with the quiet dead,
Baby, thy rest shall be.
O, many a weary wight,
Weary of life and light,
Would fain lie down with thee!

Flee, little tender nursling,
Flee to thy grassy nest;
There the first flowers shall blow,
The first pure flakes of snow
Shall fall upon thy breast.

Peace! peace! the little bosom
    Labors with shortening breath.
Peace! peace! that tremulous sigh
Speaks his departure nigh;
    Those are the damps of death.

I've seen thee in thy beauty,
    A thing all health and glee;
But never, then, wert thou
So beautiful as now,
    Baby, thou seemest to me;

Thine upturned eyes glazed over,
    Like harebells wet with dew,
Already veiled and hid
By the convulsèd lid,
    Their pupils darkly blue;

Thy little mouth half open,
    The soft lip quivering,
As if, like summer air

Ruffling the rose leaves, there
    Thy soul were fluttering.

Mount up, immortal essence!
    Young spirit, hence. depart!
And is *this* death? Dread thing!
If such thy visiting,
    How beautiful thou art.

O, I could gaze forever
    Upon that waxen face,
So passionless! so pure!
The little shrine was sure
    An angel's dwelling-place.

Thou weepest, childless mother!
    Ay, weep; 'twill ease thine heart:
He was thy first-born son—
Thy first, thine only one;
    'Tis hard from him to part.

'Tis hard to lay thy darling
  Deep in the damp, cold earth;
His empty crib to see,
His silent nursery,
  Late singing with his mirth;

To meet again, in slumber,
  His small mouth's rosy kiss,
Then — wakened with a start
By thine own throbbing heart —
  His twining arms to miss;

And then to lie and weep,
  And think, the livelong night,
(Feeling thine own distress
With accurate greediness,)
  Of every past delight;

Of all his winning ways,
  His pretty, playful smiles,
His joy at sight of thee,

His tricks, his mimicry,
    And all his little wiles.

O, these are recollections
    Round mothers' hearts that cling!
That mingle with the tears
And smiles of after years,
    With oft awakening.

But thou wilt then, fond mother,
    In after years, look back
(Time brings such wondrous easing)
With sadness and unpleasing,
    Even on this gloomy track.

Thou'lt say, "My first-born blessing,
    It almost broke my heart,
When thou wert forced to go;
And yet, for thee, I know
    'Twas better to depart.

"God took thee in his mercy,
    A lamb untasked, untried;
He fought the fight for thee,
He won the victory,
    And thou art sanctified.

"I look around, and see
    The evil ways of men,
And O, belovéd child!
I'm more than reconciled
    To thy departure then.

"The little arms that clasped me,
    The innocent lips that prest,
Would they have been as pure
Till now, as when of yore
    I lulled thee on my breast?

"Now, like a dew-drop shrined
    Within a crystal stone,
Thou'rt safe in heaven, my dove!

Safe with the Source of love,
The everlasting One!

"And when the hour arrives
From flesh that sets me free,
Thy spirit may await,
The first at heaven's gate,
To meet and welcome me."

SUNDAY EVENING.

I SAT, last Sunday evening,
From sunset even till night,
At the open casement, watching
The day's departed light

Such hours to me are holy,—
Holier than tongue can tell;
They fall on my heart like dew
On the parched heather-bell.

The sun had shone bright all day;
His setting was brighter still;
But there sprang up a lovely air
As he dropped the western hill.

The fields and lanes were swarming
With holyday folks in their best,
Released from their six days' cares
By the seventh day's peace and rest.

I heard the light-hearted laugh,
The trampling of many feet;
I saw them go merrily by,
And to me the sight was sweet.

There's a sacred, soothing sweetness,
A pervading spirit of bliss,
Peculiar from all other times,
In a Sabbath eve like this.

Methinks, though I knew not the day,
Nor beheld those glad faces, yet all

Would tell me that Nature was keeping
  Some solemn festival.

The steer and the steed in their pastures
  Lie down with a look of peace,
As if they knew 'twas commanded
  That this day their labor should cease.

The lark's vesper song is more thrilling,
  As he mounts to bid heaven good night;
The brook sings a quieter tune,
  The sun sets in livelier light;

The grass, the green leaves, and the flowers,
  Are tinged with more exquisite hues;
More odorous incense from out them
  Steams up with the evening dews.

So I sat, last Sunday evening,
  Musing on all these things,
With that quiet gladness of spirit
  No thought of this world brings.

I watched the departing glory,
Till its last red streak grew pale,
And earth and heaven were woven
In twilight's dusky veil.

Then the lark dropped down to his mate,
By her nest on the dewy ground,
And the stir of human life
Died away to a distant sound

All sounds died away — the light laugh,
The far footstep, the merry call —
To such stillness, the pulse of one's heart
Might have echoed a rose leaf 's fall.

And, ty little and little, the darkness
Waved wider its sable wings,
Till the nearest objects and largest
Became shapeless, confuséd things.

And, at last, all was dark ; then I felt
A cold sadness steal over my heart ;

And I said to myself, "Such is life!
  So its hopes and its pleasures depart!

"And when night comes, — the dark night, —
  What remaineth, beneath the sun,
Of all that was lovely and loved?
  Of all we have learned and done?

"When the eye waxeth dim, and the ear
  To sweet music grows dull and cold;
And the fancy burns low, and the heart —
  O heavens! *can* the heart grow old?

"Then what remaineth of life
  But the lees, with bitterness fraught?
What then?" — but I checked as it rose,
  And rebukéd, that weak, wicked though

And I lifted mine eyes up, and lo!
  An answer was written on high,
By the finger of God himself,
  In the depths of the dark blue sky

There appeared a sign in the east;
  A bright, beautiful, fixéd star!
And I looked on its steady light,
  Till the evil thoughts fled afar:

And the lesser lights of heaven
  Shone out with their pale, soft rays,
Like the calm, unearthly comforts
  Of a good man's latter days;

And there came up a sweet perfume
  From the unseen flowers below,
Like the savor of virtuous deeds,
  Of deeds done long ago;

Like the memory of well-spent time,
  Of things that were holy and dear;
Of friends "departed this life
  In the Lord's faith and fear."

So the burden of darkness was taken
  From my soul, and my heart felt light:

And I laid me down to slumber
  With peaceful thoughts that night.

LITTLE LEONARD'S LAST "GOOD NIGHT."

"Good night! good night! I go to sleep,"*
  Murmured the little child;
And O, the ray of heaven that broke
On the sweet lips that faintly spoke
  That soft "good night," and smiled!

That angel smile! that loving look
  From the dim, closing eyes!
The peace of that pure brow! But there —
Ay, on that brow, so young, so fair —
  An awful shadow lies.

* The real exclamation of a child, as he died.

4

The gloom of evening, of the boughs
  That o'er yon window wave —
Nay, nay, within these silent walls
A deeper, darker shadow falls,
  The twilight of the grave —

The twilight of the grave; for still
  Fast comes the fluttering breath;
One fading smile, *one* look of love,
A murmur, as from brooding dove,
  "Good night:" — and this is death!

O, who hath called thee "terrible"?
  Mild angel! most benign!
Could mother's fondest lullaby
Have laid to rest more blissfully
  That sleeping babe, than thine?

Yet *this is death* — the doom for all
  Of Adam's race decreed;
"But this poor lamb, this little one,

What had the guiltless creature done?"
  Unhappy heart, take heed!

Though HE is merciful as just
  Who hears that fond appeal,
He will not break the bruiséd reed,
He will not search the wounds that bleed;
  He only wounds to heal.

"Let little children come to me,"
  He cried, and to his breast
Folded them tenderly; to-day
He calls thine unshorn lamb away
  To that securest rest.

A FAIR PLACE AND PLEASANT.

A fair place and pleasant, this same world of ours.
Who says there are serpents 'mong all the swee
flowers?
Who says every blossom we pluck has its thorn?
Pho! pho! laugh these musty old sayings to scorn.

If you roam to the tropics for flowers rich and rare,
No doubt there are serpents, and deadly ones, there
If none but the rose will content ye, 'tis true
Ye may get sundry scratches, and ugly ones too.

But pr'ythee look there; could a serpent find room
In that close-woven moss, where those violet
bloom?
And reach me that woodbine, (you'll get it with
ease;)
Now, wiseacre, where are the thorns, if you please

say there are angels in every spot,
'hough our dim, earthly vision discerneth them not;
'hat they're guardians, assigned to the least of us all
y Him who takes note if a sparrow but fall;

'hat they're aye flitting near us, around us, above,
n missions of kindness, compassion, and love;
'hat they're glad when we're happy, disturbed at
our tears,
istressed at our weaknesses, failings, and fears;

'hat they care for the least of our innocent joys,
'hough we're cozened, like children, with trifles
and toys;
nd can lead us to bloom-beds, and lovely ones too,
Vhere snake never harbored, and thorn never grew

THE MARINER'S HYMN.

Launch thy bark, mariner!
  Christian, God speed thee!
Let loose the rudder-bands;
  Good angels lead thee!
Set thy sails warily,
  Tempests will come;
Steer thy course steadily,
  Christian, steer home!

Look to the weather-bow,
  Breakers are round thee;
Let fall the plummet now,
  Shallows may ground thee.
Reef in the foresail, there!
  Hold the helm fast!
So; let the vessel wear;
  There swept the blast.

"What of the night, watchman?
  What of the night?"
"Cloudy; all quiet;
  No land yet; all's right."
Be wakeful, be vigilant;
  Danger may be
At an hour when all seemeth
  Securest to thee.

How! gains the leak so fast?
  Clear out the hold;
Hoist up thy merchandise,
  Heave out thy gold.
There! let the ingots go;
  Now the ship rights;
Hurra! the harbor 's near!
  Lo, the red lights!

Slacken not sail yet
  At inlet or island;
Straight for the beacon steer,

Straight for the high land;
Crowd all thy canvass on,
Cut through the foam;
Christian! cast anchor now,
Heaven is thy home!

"THERE IS A TONGUE IN EVERY LEAF."

There is a tongue in every leaf,
A voice in every rill;
A voice that speaketh every where, —
In flood and fire, through earth and air, —
A tongue that's never still.

'Tis the great Spirit, wide diffused
Through every thing we see,
That with our spirits communeth
Of things mysterious — life and death,
Time and eternity.

I see him in the blazing sun,
  And in the thunder-cloud ;
I hear him in the mighty roar
That rushes through the forest hoar
  When winds are piping loud.

I see him, hear him, every where ;
  In all things, — darkness, light,
Silence, and sound ; but, most of all,
When slumber's dusky curtains fall,
  At the dead hour of night.

I *feel* him in the silent dews
  By grateful earth betrayed ;
I *feel* him in the gentle showers,
The soft south wind, the breath of flowers,
  The sunshine and the shade.

And yet — ungrateful that I am ! —
  I've turned in sullen mood
From all these things, whereof He said,

When the great work was finishéd,
  That they were "very good"!

My sadness on the fairest things
  Fell like unwholesome dew;
The darkness that encompassed me,
The gloom I felt so palpably,
  Mine own dark spirit threw.

Yet He was patient, slow to wrath,
  Though every day provoked
By selfish, pining discontent,
Acceptance cold, or negligent,
  And promises revoked.

And still the same rich feast was spread
  For my insensate heart. —
Not always so; I woke again,
To join creation's rapturous strain;
  "O Lord! how good Thou art!"

The clouds drew up, the shadows fled,
  The glorious sun broke out;
And love, and hope, and gratitude,
Dispelled that miserable mood
  Of darkness and of doubt.

THE BROKEN BRIDGE.

It was a lovely autumn morn,
  So indistinctly bright,
So many-hued, so misty, clear,
So blent the glittering atmosphere,
  A web of opal light!

The morning mist, from the hill top,
  Sailed off, (a silvery flake,)
But still in the under-vale it lay,
Where the trees peered out like islands gray,
Seen dimly, at the dawn of day,
  On a waveless, pearly lake

And again, when we reached the woody rise
  That Boldre church doth crown,
The filmy shroud was wafted by,
And, rejoicing in his victory,
  The dazzling sun looked down.

We reached the church, a two-mile walk,
  Just as the bell begun;
Only the clerk was stationed there,
And one old man with silver hair,
  Who warmed him in the sun.

A gravestone for his seat, one hand
  On his old staff leaned he;
The other fondly dalliéd
With the bright curls of a young head
  That nestled on his knee

The child looked up in the old man's face,
  Looked up and laughed the while.
Methought 'twas a beautiful sight to see

The reflected light of its innocent glee,
(Like a sunbeam on a withered tree,)
  In the old man's quiet smile.

That simple group well harmonized
  With the surrounding scene;
The old gray church, with its shadows deep,
Where the dead seemed hushed in sounder sleep;
And all beyond, where the sun shone bright,
Touching the tombstones with golden light,
  And the graves with emerald green.

And a redbreast from the elms hard by
  His joyous matins sung;
That music wild contrasted well
With the measured sound of the old church-bell,
  In the low, square tower that swung.

I looked, and listened, and listened still,
  But word spake never a one;
And I started like one awakenéd

From a trance, when my young companion s
"Let's walk till the bell has done."

So we turned away by the shady path
That winds down the pleasant hill;
Leaving the churchyard to the right
High up, it brought us soon in sight
Of the clear spring, so sparkling bright,
That turns old Hayward mill.

A lovely scene! but not therefore
Young Edmund's choice, I doubt;
No; rather that with barbéd snare,
For sport, he oft inveigled there
The perch and speckled trout.

Stopped was the busy mill-wheel now,
Snareless the rippling brook;
And up the finny people leaped,
As if they knew that danger slept;
And Edmund! he had well-nigh wept
For lack of line and hook.

"Look, what a fish! the same, I'll swear,
That I hooked yesterday:
He's a foot long from head to tail;
The fellow tugged like any whale,
And broke my line: it's very true,
Though you laugh, miss! you always do
At every thing I say."

"Nay, gentle coz! I did but smile;
But — *was* he a foot long?"
"Ay, more, a foot and half — near two
There, there, there's no convincing *you*;
One might as well to an old shoe
Go whistle an old song."

"Gramercy, coz! I only asked,
In admiration strong."
"Ay, but you look at one so queer;
O, that I had my tackle here,
You should soon see; well, never fear,
I'll have him yet ere long."

"Ay, doubtless; but, dear Edmund! now
  Be murderous thoughts far hence.
This is a day of peace and rest,
And should diffuse in every breast
  Its holy influence."

Such desultory chat we held,
  Still idly sauntering on
Towards the old crazy bridge, that led
Across the stream by the mill-head;
  "Heyday!" said I, "'tis gone!"

And gone it was; but planks and piles
  Lay there, a fresh-brought load;
And, till a better bridge was made,
Flat stones across the brook were laid,
  So one might pass dryshod.

One with firm foot and steady eye,
  Dryshod might pass the brook;
But now, upon the farther side,

A woman and a child we spied,
And those slippery stones the woman eyed
  With vexed and angry look.

And the child stood there — a pretty boy;
  Some seven years old looked he;
Limber and lithe as a little fawn;
And I marveled much that he sprang not on
  With a boy's activity.

But his head hung down like a dew-bent flower,
  And he stood there helplessly;
And the woman (an old ill-favored crone)
Scowled at him, and said, in a sharp, cross tone,
  "You're always a plague to me!"

"What ails you, my little man?" said I;
  "Such a light, free thing as you
Should bound away, like a nimble deer,
From stone to stone, and be over here
  Before one could well count two."

The child looked up. To my dying day,
  That look will haunt my mind.
The woman looked, too, and she tuned her throat,
As she answered me, to a softer note,
  And says she, "The poor thing 's blind.

"His father (who's dead) was my sister's son;
  Last week his mother died, too.
He's but a weakly thing, you see;
Yet the parish has put him upon me,
  Who am but ill to do.

"And his mother made him more helpless still
  Than else he might have been;
For she nursed him up like a little lamb
That in winter's time had lost its dam:
  Such love was never seen!

"To be sure, he was her only one;
  A helpless thing, you see;
So she toiled and toiled to get him bread,

And to keep him neat: 'twas her pride, she said.
Well, 'tis a hard thing, now she's dead,
To have him thrown on me.

"And now we shall be too late for church,
For he can't get over, not he;
I thought the old bridge did well enough,
But they're always at some altering stuff,
Hindering poor folks, like we."

I looked about, but from my side
Edmund was gone already;
And, with the child clasped carefully,
Across the stream back bounded he,
With firm foot, light and steady.

And the woman," said I, "won't you help her too
Look, there she waits the while."
"Hang her, old cat! if I do," quoth he,
"To souse her into the midst 'twill be!"
For my life I could not but smile.

So we left her to cross as best she might,
  And I turned to the sightless child ;
His old white hat was wound about
With a rusty crape, and fair curls waved out
  On a brow divinely mild.

And the tears still swam in his large blue eyes,
  And hung on his sickly cheek ;
Those eyes, with their clouded vacancy,
That looked *toward*, but not *at* me,
Yet spoke to my heart more touchingly
  Than the brightest could ever speak.

I took his little hand in mine,
  ('Twas a delicate, small hand,)
And the poor thing soon crept close to me,
With a timid familiarity
  No heart could e'er withstand.

By this time the woman had hobbled up ;
  "Ah, Goody ! what, safe ashore ?"

Quoth Edmund, "I knew without help from me
You'd paddle across." Askance looked she,
But spake not a word; so in company
We moved on to church all four

But I felt the child's hand, still held in mine,
With a shrinking dread compressed;
"Do you love to go to church?" I said;
"Yes," and he hung down his little head,
"But I love the churchyard best."

"The churchyard, my pretty boy? And why?
Come, tell me why, and how."
"Because—because"—and the poor thing
Sobbed out the words, half whispering,
"'Cause mammy is there now."

Feelings too deep for utterance
Thrilled me a moment's space
At last, "My little friend," said I,
"She's gone to live with God on high,
In heaven, his dwelling-place.

"And if you're good, and pray to him,
  And tell the truth alway,
And bear all hardships patiently,
You'll go there too." "But when?" said he
  "Shall I go there to-day?"

"Nay, you must wait till God is pleased
  To call you to his rest."
"When will that be?" he asked again.
"Perhaps not yet, my child." "O, then
  I love the churchyard best."

And to the churchyard we were come,
  And close to the church door;
And the little hand I held in mine,
Still held, loath was I to resign;
And, from that hour, the face so mild,
And the soft voice of that orphan child,
  Have haunted me evermore.

THE MOTHER'S LAMENT

My child was beautiful and brave —
  An opening flower of spring!
He moulders in a distant grave —
  A cold, forgotten thing.
Forgotten! Ay, by all but me,
As e'en the best beloved must be
    Farewell, farewell, my dearest

Methinks 't had been a comfort now
  To have caught his parting breath;
Had I been near, from his damp brow
  To wipe the dews of death;
With one long, lingering kiss, to close
His eyelids for the last repose.
    Farewell, farewell, my dearest!

I little thought such wish to prove,
  When, cradled on my breast,

With all a mother's cautious love
  His sleeping lids I pressed.
Alas! alas! his dying head
Was pillowed on a colder bed.
    Farewell, farewell, my dearest!

They told me victory's laurels wreathed
  His youthful temples round;
That "victory" from his lips was breathed,
  The last exulting sound:
Cold comfort to a mother's ear,
That longed his *living* voice to hear.
    Farewell, farewell, my dearest!

E'en so thy gallant father died,
  When thou, poor orphan child!
A helpless prattler at my side,
  My widowed grief beguiled.
But now, bereaved of all in thee,
What earthly voice shall comfort me?
    Farewell, farewell, my dearest!

"IT IS NOT DEATH"

It is not Death — it is not Death,
  From which I shrink with coward fear;
It is that I must leave behind
    All I love here.

It is not Wealth — it is not Wealth,
  That I am loath to leave behind;
Small store to me (yet all I crave)
    Hath fate assigned.

It is not Fame — it is not Fame,
  From which it will be pain to part;
Obscure my lot; but mine was still
    An humble heart.

It is not Health — it is not Health,
  That makes me fain to linger here;
For I have languished on in pain
    This many a year.

It is not Hope — it is not Hope,
From which I cannot turn away;
O, earthly Hope has cheated me
This many a day!

But there are Friends — but there are Friends,
To whom I could not say "Farewell,"
Without a pang more hard to bear
Than tongue can tell.

But there's a thought — but there's a thought
Will arm me with that pang to cope;
Thank God! we shall not part like those
Who have no hope.

And some are gone — and some are gone —
Methinks they chide my long delay —
With whom, it seemed, my very life
Went half away.

But we shall meet — but we shall meet —
Where parting tears shall never flow;

And, when I think thereon, almost
I long to go.

The Savior wept — the Savior wept
O'er him he loved — corrupting clay!
But then He spake the word, and Death
Gave up his prey!

A little while — a little while —
And the dark Grave shall yield its trust;
Yea, render every atom up
Of human dust.

What matters then — what matters then —
Who earliest lays him down to rest?
Nay, "to depart, and be with Christ,"
Is surely best.

ON THE NEAR PROSPECT OF LEAVING HOME. 1838.

Farewell, farewell, beloved home!
 Haven of rest! a long farewell;
Where'er my weary footsteps roam,
 With thee shall faithful memory dwell.

They tell me other bowers will rise
 As fair, in fancy's future view;
They little think what tender ties,
 Dear home! attach my heart to you!

Their happy childhood has not played,
 Like mine, beneath thy sheltering roof;
Thou hast not fostered, in thy shade,
 Their after years of happier youth.

They cannot know, they have not proved,
 The sympathies that make thee dear;

They have not here possessed and loved:
  They have not lost and sorrowed here.

In all around, they cannot see
  Relics of hopes, and joys o'ercast;
They have not learned to live, like me,
  On recollections of the past.

To watch (as misers watch their gold)
  Tree, shrub, or flower, (frail, precious trust!)
Planted and reared in days of old,
  By hands now mouldering in the dust;

To sanctify peculiar places,
  Associated in memory's glass,
With circumstances, times, and faces,
  That like a dream before me pass.

These are the feelings, *this* the band,
  Dear home! that knits my heart to thee;
No heart but mine can understand
  How strong that secret sympathy

THE LADYE'S BRYDALLE.

"Come hither, come hither, my little foot-page!
  And beare to my gaye Ladye
This ringe of the good red gowde, and be sure
  Rede well what she tellethe to thee.

"And take tent, little Page, if my Ladye's cheeke
  Be with watchinge and weepinge pale;
If her locks are unkempt, and her bonnie eyes redde;
  And come backe and telle me thye tale.

"And marke, little Page, when thou showest the
    ringe,
  If she snatchethe it hastelye,
If the red blude mount up her slendere throate
  To her forehedde of ivorye.

"And take good heede if, for gladness or griefe,
  It chaungethe my Ladye's cheere;

You shalle know by her eyes; if their lichte laugh oute
  Through the miste of a startlinge teare,

"(Like the Summer sunne thro' a morninge cloude,)
  There needethe no furthere tokenne,
That mye Ladye brighte, to her owne true Knighte,
  Hath keepit her faithe unbrokenne.

"Now ride, little Page, for the sunne peeres oute
  Owre the rimme of the eastern heavenne,
And backe thou must bee, with thy tidinges, to mee,
  Ere the shadow falles far at evenne."

Awaye, and awaye! and he's farre on his waye,
  The little foot-page alreddye;
For he's backed on his Lordes own gallante graye,
  That steede so swift and steddye.

But the Knighte stands there like a charmedde manne,

Watchinge, with eare and eye,
The clatteringe speede of his noble steede,
That swifte as the windes doth flye.

But the windes and the lichtninges are loitererres alle
To the glaunce of a luver's mynde;
And Sir Alwynne, I trow, had thocht Bonnybelle slowe,
Had her fleetnesse outstrippit the winde.

Beseemed to him, that the sunne once more
Had stayedde his course that daye;
Never sicke manne longed for morninge licht
As Sir Alwynne for eveninge graye.

But the longeste daye must ende at laste,
And the brighteste sunne must sette;
Where stayde Sir Alwynne at peepe of dawne,
There at even he stayethe him yette.

And he spyethe at laste — "Not soe, not soe
'Tis a small graye cloude, Sir Knighte,
That risethe up, like a courser's hedde,
On that borderre of gowden lichte."

"Bot harke! bot harke! for I heare it nowe;
'Tis the comynge of Bonnybelle!"
"Not soe, Sir Knighte; from that rockye height
'Twas a clatteringe stone that felle."

'That slothfulle boye! but I'll think no more
Of him and that lagginge jade to-daye."
"Righte, righte, Sir Knighte!" "Nay, now, by this lichte,
Here cometh my Page and my gallante graye!

"Howe nowe, little Page! ere thou lichtest downe,
Speake but one worde out hastylye;
Little Page, haste thou seen mye Ladye luve?
Hathe mye Ladye keepit her faithe with me?"

"I've seene thye Ladye luve, Sir Knighte,
  And welle hathe she keepit her faithe with thee."
"Lichte downe, lichte downe, mye trustye Page!
  A berrye browne barbe shall thy guerdon be.

"Telle on, telle on; was mye Ladye's cheeke
  Pale as the lilye, or rosye redde?
Did she put the ringe on her finger smalle?
  And what was the very firste worde she sedde?"

"Pale was thye Ladye's cheeke, Sir Knighte,
  Blent with no streake of the rosye redde;
I put the ringe on her finger smalle,
  But there is no voice amongste the dedde."

* * * * *

There are torches hurryinge to and froe
  In Raeburne Towerre to-nighte;
And the chapelle dothe glowe with lampes alsoe,
  As if for a brydalle ryte.

But where is the Bryde? and the Brydegroome
where?
And where is the holye Prieste?
And where are the guestes that shoulde biddenne be,
To partake of the marriage feast?

The Bryde from her chamberre descendethe slowe,
And the Brydegroome her hand hath ta'en;
And the guestes are mette, and the holy Prieste
Precedethe the marriage traine.

The Bryde is the fayre Maude Winstanlye,
And Dethe her stern Brydegroome;
And her father followes his onlye childe
To her mothere's yawninge tombe.

An agedde manne! and a wofulle manne!
And a heavye moane makes he;
"Mye childe! mye childe! mine onlye childe!
Would God I had dyedde for thee!"

An agedde manne, those white haires telle,
  And that bendedde back and knee;
Yette a stalwart Knighte, at Tewkesburye fighte,
  Was Sir Archibalde Winstanlye!

'Tis a movinge thinge to see the teares
  Wrunge oute frae an agedde eye,
Seldome and slowe, like the scantye droppes
  Of a fountaine that 's neere a drye.

'Tis a sorrye sighte to see graye haires
  Brocht downe to the grave with sorrowe!
Youth lukes thro' the cloude of the presente daye
  For a goldonne gleame to-morrowe.

But the palsyedde hedde, and the feeble knees,
  Berefte of earthlye staye! . . . .
God help thee nowe, old Winstanlye!
  Gude Christians for thee praye!

Bot manye a voice in that burialle traine
  Breathes gloomily aparte,

"Thou hadst not been childeless nowe, olde manne,
But for thine owne harde hearte!"

And many a mayde, who strewethe floweres
Afore the Ladye's biere,
Weepes oute, "Thou hadst not dyede sweet Maude
If Alwynne had beene heere!"

* * * * * *

What solemne chaunte ascendethe slowe?
What voices peale the straine?
The Monkes of St. Switholm's Abbaye neare
Have mette the funeralle traine

They hold their landes, full manye a roode,
From the Knightes of Raeburne Towerre;
And everre when Dethe doth claime his preye
From within that lordlye bowerre,

Then come the holye Fatheris forthe,
The shrowdedde corse to meete

And see it laide in [illegible] grave
  With requiem sadde and sweete.

And nowe they turne, and leade the waye
  To that laste home so nigh,
Where alle the race of Winstanlye
  In dust and darkness lye.

The holye altarre blazethe brighte
  With waxen taperres high;
Elsewhere, in dimme and doubtfulle lichte
  Dothe alle the chapelle lye.

Huge, undefinedde shadowes falle
  From pillare and from tombe;
And manye a grimme olde monumente
  Lookes ghastelye through the gloome.

And many a rustye shirt of maile
  The eye maye scantlye trace;
And crestedde helmette, blacke and barred,
  That grinnes with sterne grimace.

Bannerre and scutcheon from the walles
  Wave in the cald nighte aire ;
Gleames oute their gorgeous heraldrye
  In the entering torches' glare.

For nowe the mourninge companye
  Beneathe that archedde doore,
Beare in the lovelye, lifelesse claye,
  Shall passe thereoute no more.

And up the soundinge aisle ye stille
  Their solemne chaunte may heare,
Tille 'neath that blazonned catafalque
  They gentlye reste the biere.

Then ceasethe everye sounde of life ;
  So deepe that awfulle hushe,
Ye heare from yon freshe-opennedde vaulte
  The hollowe deathe-windo rushe.

Backe from the biere the mournerres all
  Retire a little space ;

Alle bot that olde bereavedde manne,
  Who takethe there his place

Beside the dedde: but none may see
  The workinges of his mynde;
So lowe upon that sunkenne breste
  Is that graye hedde declinede.

* * * * * *

The masse is saide; they raise the dedde;
  The palle is flunge aside;
And soone that coffinned lovelyenesse
  The darksome pit shalle hide.

It gapeth close at hande. Deep downe
  Ye may the coffinnes see
(By the lampe's dull glare, freshe kindledde
  Of many a Winstanlye.

And the gildedde nails on one looke brighte,
  And the velvette of cramoisie,

She hathe not laine there a calenderre yeere,
  The laste Dame Winstanlye.

"There's roome for thee heere, O daughter deere!"
  Methinkes I heare her saye;
"There's roome for thee, Maude Winstanlye;
  Come downe, make no delaye."

And, from the vaulte, two grimlye armes
  Upraised, demaunde the dedde! . .
Hark! hark! 'tis the tramp of a rushinge steede!
  'Tis the clanke of an armedde tredde!

There's an armedde hedde at the chapelle doore;
  And, in armoure all bedighte,
In coal-blacke steele, from hedde to heele,
  In steppes an armedde Knighte!

And uppe the aisle, with heavy tredde,
  Alone advauncethe he;
To barre his waye dothe none essaye
  Of the fun'ralle companye.

And never a voice amongst them alle
  Doth aske who he mote be;
Nor why his armedde steppe disturbes
  That sadde solemnitye.

Yette manye an eye, with fixedde stare,
  Dothe sternelye on him frowne;
Bot none may trace the stranger's face—
  He weares his vizorre downe.

He speakes no worde, bot waves his hande,
  And straighte theye alle obeye;
And ev'rye soule that standethe there
  Falles backe to make him waye.

He passethe on; no hande dothe stirre;
  His steppe the onlye sounde;
He passethe on, and signes them sette
  The coffinne on the grounde.

A momente gazinge downe thereonne,
  With foldedde armes dothe staye;

Then stooppinge, with one mightye wrench
  He teares the lidde awaye.

Then risethe a confusedde sounde,
  And some half forwarde starte,
And murmurre, "Sacriledge!" And some
  Bear hastilye aparte

The agedde Knighte, at that straunge sighte
  Whose consciousnesse hathe fledde;
Bot signe nor sounde disturbethe him
  Who gazethe on the dedde.

And seemethe sune, as that faire face
  Dothe alle exposedde lye,
As if its holye calme o'erspredde
  The frowninge faces bye.

And nowe, beside the virginne corse
  Downe kneeles the straunger Knighte,
And backe his vizorrede helme he throwes,
  Bot not in openne sighte;

For to the pale, colde, clammy face,
  His owne he stoopethe lowe;
And kissethe firste the bludelesse cheeke,
  And then the marble browe.

Then, to the dedde lippes gluede, so long
  The livinge lippes do stay,
As if in that sadde silente kisse
  The soule had paste awaye.

Bot suddenne, from that mortal trance,
  As with a desp'rate straine,
Up! up! he springes — his armoure ringes —
  His vizorre's downe againe.

With many a flourre, her weepinge maydes
  The Ladye's shroude have dressed;
And one white rose is in the faulde
  That veiles her whiterre breste.

One gowden ringlette on her browe
  (Escapedde forthe) dothe straye;

So on a wreathe of driftedde snowe
  The wintrye sunbeames playe.

The mailedde hande hath ta'en the rose
  From offe that breste so fayre;
The faulchion's edge, from that pale hedde,
  Hath shorne that gowden haire.

One heavye sigh! — the first and last —
  One deepe and stifledde groane!
A few longe strides, a clange of hoofes,
  And the armedde stranger 's gone!

SONNET. 1818.

DARK rolling clouds in wild confusion driven,
Obscure the full-orbed moon. In all the heaven,
One only star (the appointed evening light)
Beams mildly forth ; like friendly Pharo bright,
That, kindled on some towering summit, streams
Wide o'er the ocean-paths. Its far-off beams
First seen by him who on the silent deck
Paces his lonely watch, — a glimmering speck
Doubtful in distance. But his homeward eye
Is keen the faithful beacon to descry;
And mine, like his, impatient to explore
(With friends and kindred thronged) the distant shore,
Is fixed on that lone star, whose lovely ray
Points to a happier home the heavenward way.

SONNET. 1821.

STAY, flaming chariot! fiery coursers, stay;
  Soft gleams of setting sunshine, that doth cast
  A lustrous line along the dark, wide waste!
O, wherefore must ye fade so swift away?
Wherefore, O wherefore, at the close of day
  Shine out so glorious, when night's sable pall
  Will drop around so soon, and cover all?
Beautiful beam! bright traveller! stay, O, stay!
And let my spirit on your parting ray
  Glide from this world of error, doubt, distress,
  (O, I am weary of its emptiness,)
To happier worlds, where there is peace for aye
Peace! less abiding here than Noah's dove;
When we shall never part from those we love.

GRACIOUS RAIN.

The east wind had whistled for many a day,
 Sere and wintry, o'er Summer's domain;
And the sun, muffled up in a dull robe of gray,
 Looked sullenly down on the plain.

The butterfly folded her wings as if dead,
 Or awaked ere the full-destined time;
Every flower shrank inward, or hung down its head
 Like a young heart frost-nipped in its prime.

I, too, shrank and shivered, and eyed the cold earth,
 The cold heaven, with comfortless looks;
And I listened in vain for the summer bird's mirth,
 And the music of rain-plenished brooks.

But, lo! while I listened, down heavily dropped
 A few tears from a low-sailing cloud;

Large and few they descended, then thickened, then
stopped,
Then poured down abundant and loud.

O the rapture of beauty, of sweetness, of sound,
That succeeded that soft, gracious rain!
With laughter and singing the valleys rang round,
And the little hills shouted again.

The wind sank away like a sleeping child's breath,
The pavilion of clouds was upfurled;
And the sun, like a spirit triumphant o'er death,
Smiled out on this beautiful world.

On this "*beautiful world*" such a change had been
wrought
By these few blessed drops. O! the same
On some cold, stony heart might be worked, too
methought,
Sunk in guilt, but not senseless of shame.

If a few virtuous tears, by the merciful shed,
 Touched its hardness, perhaps the good grain
That was sown there and rooted, though long *seeming* dead,
 Might shoot up and flourish again.

And the smile of the virtuous, like sunshine from heaven,
 Might chase the dark clouds of despair;
And remorse, when the rock's flinty surface was riven,
 Might gush out and soften all there.

O! to work such a change — by God's grace to recall
 A poor soul from the death sleep! to this, —
To this joy, that the angels partake, — what were all
 That the worldly and sensual call bliss?

THE WELCOME HOME. 1820.

Hark, hark, they're come! those merry bells,
That peal their joyous welcome swells;
And many hearts are swelling high
With more than joy — with ecstasy!

And many an eye is straining now
Toward that good ship, that sails so slow;
And many a look toward the land
They cast, upon that deck who stand.

Flow, flow, ye tides! ye languid gales,
Rise, rise, and fill their flagging sails!
Ye tedious moments, fly, begone,
And speed the blissful meeting on.

Impatient watchers! happy ye,
Whose hope shall soon be certainty;
Happy, thrice happy! soon to strain
Fond hearts to kindred hearts again.

Brothers and sisters, children, mother —
All, all restored to one another!
All, all returned; and are there none
To *me* restored, returned? Not one.

Far other meeting *mine* must be
With friends long lost; far other sea
Than thou, O restless ocean! flows
Between us — one that never knows

Ebb-tide or flood; a stagnant sea;
Time's gulf; its shore, eternity!
No voyager from that shadowy bourn
With chart or sounding may return.

There, there *they* stand — the loved! the lost!
They beckon from that awful coast!
They cannot thence return to me,
But I shall go to them. I see

E'en now, methinks, those forms so dear,
Bend smiling to invite me there.

O best beloved ! a little while,
And I obey that beckoning smile.

'Tis all my comfort, now, to know
In God's good time it shall be so ;
And yet, in that sweet hope's despite,
Sad thoughts oppress my heart to-night.

And doth the sight of others' gladness
Oppress this selfish heart with sadness?
Now Heaven forbid ! but tears will rise,
Unbidden tears, into mine eyes,

When busy thought contrasts with theirs
My fate, my feelings. Four brief years
Have winged their flight, since where they stand
I stood, and watched that parting band,

(*Then* parting hence ;) and *one*, methought,
(O human foresight ! set at nought

By God's unfathomed will!) was borne
From England, never to return.

With saddened heart, I turned to seek
Mine own belovéd home; to speak
With her who shared it of the fears
She also shared in . . It appears

But yesterday that thus we spoke;
And I can see the very look
With which she said, "I do believe
Mine eyes have ta'en their last, long leave

Of her who has gone hence to-day!"
Five months succeeding slipped away;
And, on the sixth, a deep-toned bell
Swung slow, of recent death to tell.

It tolled for her with whom, so late,
I reasoned of impending fate;
To me those solemn words who spoke
So late, with that remembered look!

And *now*, from that same steeple, swells
A joyous peal of merry bells,
Her welcome, whose approaching doom
We blindly thought — a foreign tomb!

THE NIGHT-SMELLING STOCK.

Come, look at this plant, with its narrow, pale leaves,
And its tall, slim, delicate stem,
Thinly studded with flowers! Yes, with flowers!
There they are!
Don't you see at each joint there's a little brown
star?
But, in truth, there 's no beauty in them.

So you ask why I keep it — the little, mean thing;
Why I stick it up here, just in sight;
'Tis a fancy of mine. "A strange fancy!" you say

"No accounting for tastes!" In this instance you
may;
For the flower . . . . But I'll tell you to-night.

Some six hours hence, when the lady moon
Looks down on that bastioned wall,
When the twinkling stars dance silently
On the rippling surface of the sea,
And the heavy night-dews fall,

Then meet me again in this casement niche,
On the spot where we 're standing now.
Nay, question not wherefore. Perhaps, with me,
To look on the night, and the broad, bright sea,
And to hear its majestic flow!

* * * * * *

Well, we're met here again; and the moonlight
sleeps
On the sea, and the bastioned wall;

And the flowers there below ; how the night-wind
brings
Their delicious breath on its dewy wings !
"But there's one," say you, "sweeter than all!"

"Which is it? The myrtle, or jessamine,
Or their sovereign lady, the rose?
Or the heliotrope? or the virgin's bower?—
What! neither?" O, no, 'tis some other flower,
Far sweeter than either of those.

Far sweeter! And where, think you, groweth the
plant
That exhaleth such perfumes rare?
Look about, up and down, but take care! or you'll
break,
With your elbow, that poor little thing, that's so
weak,
. . . . "Why, 'tis that smells so sweet, I declare!"

Ah ha! is it *that*? Have you found out, now,
Why I cherish that odd little fright?

"All is not gold that glitters," you know;
And it is not all worth makes the greatest show
In the glare of the strongest light.

There are *human* flowers full many, I trow,
As unlovely as that by your side,
That a common observer passeth by
With a scornful lip, and a careless eye,
In the heyday of pleasure and pride.

But move one of those to some quiet spot,
From the mid-day sun's broad glare,
Where domestic peace broods with dove-like wing;
And try if the homely, despiséd thing
May not yield sweet fragrance there.

Or wait till the days of trial come —
The dark days of trouble and woe;
When they shirk, and shut up, late so bright in the
sun;

Then turn to the little despiséd one,
  And see if 'twill serve you so.

And judge not again at a single glance,
  Nor pass sentence hastily;
There are many good things in this world of ours;
Many sweet things and rare! weeds that prove precious flowers!
  Little dreamed of by you or me.

MY EVENING

FAREWELL, bright sun! mine eyes have watched
  Thine hour of waning light;
And tender twilight! fare thee well;
  And welcome, star-crowned night!

Pale! serious! silent! with deep spell
  Lulling the heart to rest,

As lulls the mother's low, sweet song,
  The infant on her breast

Mine own belovéd hour! — mine own!
  Sacred to quiet thought,
To sacred memories, to calm joys
  With no false lustre fraught!

Mine own belovéd hour! for now,
  Methinks, with gairish day,
I shut the world out, and with those
  Long lost, or far away,

The dead, the absent, once again
  My soul holds converse free;
To such illusions, life! how dull
  Thy best reality!

The vernal nights are chilly yet,
  And cheerily and bright
The hearth still blazes, flashing round
  Its ruddy, flickering light.

"Bring in the lamp — so — set it there,
 Just show its veiléd ray,
(Leaving all else in shadowy tone,)
 Fall on my *book* — and — stay —

"Leave my work by me" — Well I love
 The needle's useful art;
'Tis unambitious, womanly,
 And mine's a woman's heart.

Not that I ply with sempstress rage,
 As if for life, or bread;
No, sooth to say, unconsciously
 Slackening the half-drawn thread,

From fingers that (as spell-bound) stop,
 Pointing the needle wrong,
Mine eyes toward the open book
 Stray oft, and tarry long.

"Stop, stop! Leave open the glass door
 Into that winter bower;"

For soon therein th' uprisen moon
  Will pour her silvery shower;

Will glitter on those glossy leaves;
  On that white pavement shine;
And dally with her eastern love,
  That wreathing jessamine.

"Thanks, Lizzy! No; there's nothing more
  Thy loving zeal can do;
Only — O yes! — that gypsy flower,*
  Set *that* beside me too."

"That Ethiop, in the China vase?"
  "Ay; set it *here;* that's right.
Shut the door after you." 'Tis done;
  I'm settled for the night.

Settled and snug; and first, as if
  The fact to ascertain,

* The night-smelling stock.

I glance around, and stir the fire,
  And trim the lamp again.

Then, dusky flower! I stoop t' inhale
  Thy fragrance. Thou art one
That wooeth not the vulgar eye,
  Nor the broad staring sun:

Therefore I love thee! (selfish love
  Such preference may be;)
That thou reservest all thy sweets,
  Coy thing! for night and me.

What sound was that? Ah, madam puss!
  I know that tender mew,
That meek white face, those sea-green eyes,
  Those whiskers, wet with dew,

To the gold glass — the greenhouse glass —
  Pressed closely from without;
Well, thou art heard; I'll let thee in,
  Though skulking home, no doubt

From lawless prowl. Ah, ruthless cat
  What evil hast thou done?
What deeds of rapine, the broad eye
  Of open day that shun?

What! not a feather plucked to-night?
  Is that what thou wouldst tell
With that soft purr, those twinkling eyes,
  And waving tail? — Well, well,

I know thee, friend! But get thee in;
  By Ranger stretch and doze;
Nay, never growl, old man! her tail
  Just whisked across thy nose;

But 'twas no act premeditate,
  Thy greatness to molest:
Then, with that long, luxurious sigh,
  Sink down again to rest;

But not before one loving look
  Towards me, with that long sigh,

Says, "Mistress mine, all's right, all's well!
  Thou'rt there, and here am *I!*"

That point at rest, we're still again;
  I on my work intent;
At least, with poring eyes, thereon
  In seeming earnest bent;

And fingers, nimble at their task,
  Mechanically true;
Tho' Heaven knows where, what scenes, the while
  My thoughts are travelling to!

Now far from earth, now over earth,
  Traversing lands and seas;
Now stringing, in a sing-song mood,
  Such idle rhymes as these;

Now dwelling on departed days—
  Ah! *that*'s no lightsome mood;
On those to come, no longer now
  Through hope's bright focus viewed;

On that which is — ay, there I pause
  No more in young delight;
But patient, grateful, well assured
  "Whatever is is right!"

And all to be is in His hands;
  O, who would take it thence?
Give me not up to mine own will,
  Merciful Providence!

Such thoughts, when other thoughts, may be
  Are darkening into gloom,
Come to me like the angel shape,
  That, standing by the tomb,

Cheered those who came to sorrow there;
  And then I see and bless
His love in all that he withholds,
  And all I still possess.

So varied, — now with book, or work,
  Or pensive reverie,

Or waking dreams, or fancy flights,
  Or scribbling vein, may be,

Or eke the pencil's cunning craft,
  Or lowly-murmured lay
To the according viola, —
  Calm evening slips away.

The felt-shod hours move swiftly on,
  Until the stroke of ten
(The accustomed signal) summons round
  My little household. Then,

The door unclosing, enters first
  That aged, faithful friend,
Whose prayer is, with her master's child
  Her blameless days to end.

The younger pair come close behind,
  But *her* dear hand alone
(Her dear old hand! now tremulous
  With palsying weakness grown)

Must reverently before me place
  The sacred book. 'Tis there;
And all our voices, all our hearts,
  Unite in solemn prayer;

In praise and thanksgiving, for all
  The blessings of the light;
In prayer, that he would keep us through
  The watches of the night.

A simple rite! and soon performed;
  Leaving, in every breast,
A heart more fittingly prepared
  For sweet, untroubled rest.

And so we part; but not before,
  Dear nurse! a kiss from thee
Imprints my brow, thy fond good-night
  To God commending me!

Amen! and may his angels keep
  Their watch around thy bed,

And guard from every hurtful thing
  Thy venerable head!

FAREWELL TO MY FRIENDS.

O, WEAR no mourning weeds for me,
  When I am laid i' the ground!
O, shed no tears for one whose sleep
  Will then be sweet and sound!

Only, my friends! do this for me:
  Pluck many a pale primrose,
And strew them on my shroud, before
  The coffin-lid they close;

And lay the heart's-ease on my breast,
  (Meet emblem there 'twill be,)
And gently place in my cold hand
  A sprig of rosemary;

And by the buried bones of those
  When living I loved best,
See me, at last, laid quietly,
  Then leave me to my rest;

And when the church-bell tolls for me
  Its last, long, hollow knell,
As the deep murmur dies away,
  Bid me a kind farewell.

And, stay; methinks there's something yet
  I'd fain request of ye;
Something I'd bid ye comfort, keep,
  Or love, for love of me.

My nurse! O, she will only wait
  Till I am fast asleep,
Then close beside me, stealthily,
  To her own pillow creep.

My dog! Poor fellow! Let him not
  Know hunger, hardship, wrong;

But he is old and feeble too;
He will not miss me long.

My dwelling! That will pass away
To those, when I am gone,
Will raze the lowly edifice
To its foundation-stone.

My flowers, that in deep lonelines
Have been as friends to me!
My garden, that, let run to waste,
A common field will be!

My picture! That's already yours —
Resemblance true, ye say:
O, true indeed! — a thing of dust,
That vanisheth away!

My harp! But that's a fairy gift
I can bequeath to none;
Unearthly hands will take it back
When the last strain is done

So, then, I've nothing more to ask,
  And little left to give;
And yet I know in your kind hearts
  My memory will live.

And so farewell, my dear good friends
  And farewell, world, to thee!
I part with some in love; with all
  In peace and charity.

THE PRIMROSE.

SAW it in my evening walk,
  A little lonely flower!
Under a hollow bank it grew,
  Deep in a mossy bower.

An oak's gnarled root, to roof the cave
  With Gothic fretwork, sprung,
Whence jewelled fern, and arum leaves,
  And ivy garlands, hung.

And from beneath came sparkling out,
  From a fallen tree's old shell,
A little rill, that clipped about
  The lady in her cell.

And there, methought, with bashful pride,
  She seemed to sit, and look
On her own maiden loveliness,
  Pale imaged in the brook

No other flower — no rival grew
  Beside my pensive maid;
She dwelt alone, a cloistered nun,
  In solitude and shade.

No sunbeam on that fairy well
  Darted its dazzling light;
Only, methought, some clear, cold star
  Might tremble there at night.

No ruffling wind could reach her there;
  No eye, methought but mine,

Or the young lambs' that came to drink,
  Had spied her secret shrine.

And there was pleasantness to me
  In such belief. Cold eyes,
That slight dear Nature's lowliness,
  Profane her mysteries.

Long time I looked and lingered there,
  Absorbed in still delight;
My spirit drank deep quietness
  In with that quiet sight.

FAREWELL TO GREECE.

Farewell forever, classic land
  Of tyrants and of slaves!
My homeward path lies far away
  Over the dark-blue waves;

Whither I go, no marble fanes
  From myrtle steeps arise,
Nor shineth there such fervid suns
  From such unclouded skies.

But yet, the earth of that dear land
  Is holier earth to me
Than thine, immortal Marathon!
  Or thine, Thermopylæ!

For there my fathers' ashes rest,
  And living hearts there be —
Warm, living hearts, and loving ones —
  That still remember me.

And O! the land that welcometh
  To *one* such bosom-shrine,
Though all beside were ruined, lost,
  That land would still be mine.

Ay, mine! albeit the breath of life
  Not there I breathéd first;

Ay, mine! albeit with barrenness
  And polar darkness cursed.

The bird that wanders all day long,
  At sunset seeks her nest:
I've wandered long; my native land!
  Now take me to thy rest.

THE THREE FRIENDS.

STANZAS ACCOMPANYING A PICTURE.

We three were loving friends! A lowly life
  Of humble peace, obscure content, we led;
Stealing away, withouten noise or strife,
  Like some small streamlet in its mossy bed.

We had our joys in common; wisdom, wit,
  And learned lore, had little share in those:
Thus, by the winter fire we used to sit,
  Or in the summer evening's warm repose,

At our sweet bowery window, opening down
  To the green grass, beneath the flowering lime,
When the deep curfew from the distant town
  Came mellowed, like the voice of olden time;

And our grave neighbor, from the barn hard by,
  The great gray owl, sailed out on soundless wings,
And the pale stars, like beams of memory,
  Brightened as twilight veiled all earthly things.

'Twas then we used to sit, as pictured *thus*—
  My pillow, as in childhood, still the same,
Those venerable knees; and close to us,
  Old Ranger, pressing oft his jealous claim.

And then I loved to feel that gentle hand
  Laid like a blessing on my head, to hear
The "auld warld" stories, ever at command,
  By all but *her* forgotten many a year

And then we talked together of the days
  We both remembered; and of those who slept;

And the old dog looked up with wistful gaze,
As if he, too, that faithful record kept.

We three were loving friends! Now one is gone,
And one, poor feeble thing! declineth fast;
And well I wot, the days are drawing on
Will find me here, the lonely and the last;

But not to tarry long; and when I go,
The stranger's hand will have dominion here,
And lay thy walls, my peaceful dwelling! low
As my last lodging in the churchyard near.

RANGER'S GRAVE.

He's dead and gone! he's dead and gone!
And the lime-tree branches wave,
And the daisy blows,
And the green grass grows,
Upon his grave.

He's dead and gone! he's dead and gone!
And he sleeps by the flowering lime,
Where he loved to lie,
When the sun was high,
In summer time.

We've laid him there, for I could not bear
His poor old bones to hide
In some dark hole,
Where rat and mole
And blind worms bide.

We've laid him there, where the blessèd air
Disports with the lovely light,
And raineth showers
Of those sweet flowers
So silver white;

Where the blackbird sings, and the wild bee's wings
Make music all day long.

And the cricket at night
(A dusky sprite!)
Takes up the song.

He loved to lie where his wakeful eye
Could keep me still in sight;
Whence a word or a sign,
Or a look of mine,
Brought him like light.

Nor a word nor sign, nor look of mine,
From under the lime-tree bough,
With bark and bound,
And frolic round,
Shall bring him now.

But he taketh his rest where he lovéd best
In the days of his life to be,
And that place will not
Be a common spot
Of earth to me.

www.ingramcontent.com/pod-product-compliance
Lightning Source LLC
LaVergne TN
LVHW021420110826
845150LV00007B/2007

* 9 7 8 1 4 2 5 5 0 8 9 4 4 *